I'll sing to you next time

Jan. 3, 2024

To Shabnum,

Pleasure seeing you again. The best to you and Misti.

Victor

I'll sing to you next time

Victor Edgar Rivera

© 2013 Victor Edgar Rivera

All rights reserved. Except for brief passages quoted in a newspaper, magazine, radio, television or internet review, no part of this book may be reproduced or transmitted, in any form, or by any means, without the written consent of the author. All inquiries regarding this book should be addressed to Victor Edgar Rivera, PO Box 493, Cherry Hill, NJ 08003. For more on the poet, visit poet-writer.com or multiculturalart.com.

ISBN-10: 0967671930
ISBN-13: 978-0-9676719-3-2

Library of Congress Control Number: 2013904417

Cover Painting: "Creativity," an original Verdadism painting by Soraida.

Book Design & Layout: Soraida Martinez.

For more on the art of Verdadism, visit soraida.com.

Printed in the U.S.A

Artist, Soraida Publishing
Post Office Box 32
Gibbsboro, NJ 08026

It's time to thank the three individuals who inspired me to
write this book. I can start by thanking Soraida for sparking the creativity in me. I can thank Mayra, my sister, for being there for me. I can thank Valerie for supporting me in many ways. To these three independent women, I say…

Olé

Word Songs

living n dying da blues / 3

Running Away Ballad / 4

Exclusion Blues / 5

Short Sweet Surreal Love Song / 6

This could be a tango / 7

This is un tango / 8

La Ballerina's Ballad / 9

My Torch Song / 10

Puerto Rican Aguinaldos

Cuando tu estas a mi lado / 13

Sin tu / 14

mantengase alegre / 15

Y cuando te miro / 16

Haiku at Various Times

Love / 19

Pride / 20

Woodbury / 21

Spirituality / 22

Speak Another language

Yo voy adonde la vida me lleve / 25

Teofilo / 26

When Ponce Parties / 27

Language is hope / 28

Swing Moods

South Jersey Diner / 31

One day in 2010 / 32

Today is the day / 33

Take it one day at a time / 34

Make it right / 35

Aspirations / 36

I'm Puerto Rican, I have issues / 37

Ranting and Raving

An absolute rant / 41

Becoming me / 42

Who is primitive / 43

What is not primitive / 44

How prejudice begins / 45

How love turns to hate / 46

How evil exists / 47

How god destroys / 48

How power turns to terror / 49

How weakness turns to power / 50

For the love of god, country and duty

In the name of god / 53

For my country / 54

It's my duty / 55

Ending it all

Dying alone ain't easy / 59

My time has come / 60

What I owe life is time / 61

Time / 62

Time to bow out now / 63

Word Songs

living n dying da blues

you gotta laugh, laugh, laugh
cause laughing's a long time coming
you gotta cry, cry, cry
cause crying's a healing feeling

laugh
laugh
laugh
cry
cry
cry

i'm just living and dying da blues
i'm just living and dying da blues

you gotta smile, smile, smile
cause smiling's a slow churning
you gotta growl, growl, growl
cause growling's a wicked hurting

smile
smile
smile
growl
growl
growl

i'm just living and dying da blues
i'm just living and dying da blues

living and dying da blues
for me
living and dying da blues
for you

Running Away Ballad

You grow more when you believe in yesterday, tomorrow, and thereafter.
You stay naïve if you know laughter, live the moment, here and after.
You can be smooth with hope or take a notion to anger.
Carry on.
Running away.

Exclusion Blues

When you know you got no power
It don't matter
You know
You don't matter

Feel the pain
You got no power
You know
You don't matter

You walking to nowhere
Far too long
You tragic like lightning
You sad like thunder
No one's listening
You just a thang

You got no power
You got no power
You know you got no power
You know
You know
You don't matter

Short Sweet Surreal Love Song

Hey lady
Touch me
Let the stars laugh
Let the moon cry

Make my day
You and me
Me and you
This moment
Side by side

For eternity for you
For eternity for me

Hey lady
Kiss me
Let the blues heave
Let the soul breathe

Right here now
You and me
Me and you
Right now
Side by side

For eternity for you
For eternity for me

Hey lady
Love me
Let the gods grieve
Let the angels sigh

Stake this time
You and me
Me and you
This day
Side by side

For eternity for you
For eternity for me

This could be a tango

I am not an angry man
I am not a long lost soul
I'm just yearning for the meaning of the mind
I'm just searching for the essence of the heart

I am not a foolish man
I am not a pitiful stooge
I'm just learning the substance of living
I'm just getting the reason for dying

Take me as I am
I am just a man

This is un tango

3 to 4
Leg over leg
Swish, swing, slide
Swish, swing, slide
Side to side to side

1 to 2
Hip on hip
Slide, stand, swirl
Slide, stand, swirl
Round and round and round

1 to 4
Cheek to cheek
Left to right
Right to left
Leg on over

Ole'

La Ballerina's Ballad

slide slide slide slide
left left left
right right right
glide glide glide glide
front front front
back back back

Take two steps over there

My torch song

Give me someone
Anyone
Anyone to be mine
Bring me somebody
Anybody
Anybody to ease my time
Give me something
Somewhere
Somewhere where I'm bound to find
Someone
Somebody
Somehow
Wanting my kind

*Puerto Rican Aguinaldos*

Cuando tu estas a mi lado

Cuando tu estas a mi lado
Yo me siento feliz
Cuando tu estas a mi lado
Yo te quiero sentir

Porque la vida es corta
Busco la mañana
Porque la vida es corta
Busco todo el día

Sin tu

Sin tu
no habría sol
para alumbrarme
no habría mundo
para fascinarme

Sin tu
no habría corazón
para buscarme
no habría labios
para encantarme

Sin tu
no habría agua
para calmarme
no habría ojos
para llorarme

Sin tu
no habría amor
para contarme
de una vida
inolvidable

mantengase alegre

mantengase alegre
esa cosa linda que va aya
ella es más bella que la luna

mantengase alegre
esa cosa linda que va aya
ella es más pura que la agua

mantengase alegre
esa cosa linda que va aya
ella es más vida que la sangre

mantengase alegre
esa cosa linda que va aya
ella es más dulce quel sabor

mantengase alegre
esa cosa linda que ya aya
ella es la vida la muerte el sol

Y cuando te miro

Y cuando te miro
me miro a mí
Pensando adonde fuimos
Pensando las cosas olvidadas
Pensando cómo vamos
Pensando quien nos espera
Y adonde iremos
Y adonde volveremos
Y adonde escapamos
Y adonde también miramos

Tú eres el mar
Yo te doy mi sol

Haiku at Various Times

Love

Haiku for you and me.
What can we make of this?
That this moment is yours and mine?

Pride

Walking up, walking down,
Steel stairs wind the way,
To broken steps, broken pride.

Woodbury

Down a serene solid street,
Lined with maples and oaks.
Why do I deserve this pleasure?

Spirituality

Bless you in the morning,
Bless you in the night,
Bless you over and over again.

Speak Another Language

Yo voy adonde la vida me lleve

Yo voy para el monte
Yo voy para el mar
Yo voy a buscar
La vida total

Yo voy para verte
Yo voy para estar
Yo voy a tocar
La vida real

Yo voy a decirte
Yo voy a pintar
Yo voy a cantar
La vida final

Teofilo

Moriste en un día claro
Sobre un sol brillante
La bandera Americana
Tu cama de Veterano
No te conocí cuando vivo
No te encuentro cuando muerto

When Ponce Parties

Plenty of plena
Platanos too
Vejigantes shimmering
Cerveza muy fria
Ismael Miranda
y Don Q

Language is hope

Dag-digity-dog-
do-ya-ya-ya-no-
dat-dis-dis-fuc-fuc-kin-world-
dun-kil-kil-my-soul-

Dag-digity-dog-
do-ya-ya-ya-no-
dat-dis-dis-fuc-fuc-kin-world
dun-kil-kil-my-soul-

Slam-slipity-slide-
is-id-id-id-so-
dem-blud-suc-kin-kin-men
cun-eat-my-mind-

Slam-slipity-slide-
is-id-id-id-so-
dem-blud-suc-kin-kin-men
cun-eat-my-mind-

Language is hope

Swing Moods

South Jersey Diner

Midnight meal is stale french-fries and greasy chicken breasts.
But I'm not here for the food.
I came to rendezvous with an old friend for fuel.

One day in 2010

What do you do when you see
someone killing herself?

Do you sit back
and watch her die?

Do you lay down
And cry cry cry?

Only a miracle
Can make you smile.

Today is the day

Today is the day
When things are going to matter
When YOU realize what matters
When you know it's not money
When you know it's not glory
When you know it's not fame
When you know it's alright
When you know it's OK
When you know it's the same
All over and over
Forever and ever
And ever the same

It may be your kiss
It may be your laughter
It may be your touch
It may be your scent
It may be the moon
It may be the sun
It may be the light
It may be the dark
It may be the moment
When your life
Minute by minute
Second by second
From the beginning
Into the end
Ends

Don't ever stop breathing

Take it one day at a time

One day at a time
That's all it takes

One day at a time
It's what you make

One day at a time
It's not tomorrow

One day at a time
It's not your sorrow

Make it right

Step over the curve
Skip to the side
Go round the corner
Take it all in stride

Don't make it spin
Don't let it bend
You can sway me back
You can let me in

Aspirations

social mobility
fiscal stability
proper society
some mental sanity
check in with vanity
not too much profanity
I aspire to be

I'm Puerto Rican, I have issues

Hey you. I have an issue with you.
When did Puerto Rico become another country,
You DUMB ASS,
Where does it say you have to speak English to be an American,
You SENSELESS SKULL.
Do you speak Chippewa?
Do you know Sioux?

Hey you. I have a quarrel with you.
I just want to settle this.
You say anthropologists call Puerto Ricans a race,
Like Negroid, Caucasoid and Mongoloid,
You BRAINLESS BODY.

Hey you. Let's compromise, me and you.
Let's classify every human being a Puerto Rican.

Do you see how idiotic that is?
Do you know what I mean?

Ranting and Raving

An Absolute Rant

You are obsolete
You do not matter
You are not here
You are inconsequential
You do not matter
You are not here
You are dispensable
You do not matter
You are not here
You are irrelevant
You do not matter
You are not here
You are unacceptable
You do not matter
You are not here
You are despicable
You do not matter
You are not here
You do not matter
You do not matter

Becoming me

Don't tell me I'm young
Don't tell me I'm old
Don't tell me my name
Don't tell me my flag
Don't tell me I'm fat
Don't tell me I'm thin
Don't tell me what's right
Don't tell me what's sin
Don't tell me what's sick
Don't tell me what's good
Don't tell me which god
Don't tell me which place
Don't tell me this day
Don't tell me that way

Who is primitive

The taliban
Who kills and maims in the name of allah
The vatican
Who steals souls in the name of god
The american government
Who stands still in blind complicity

What is not primitive

Aboriginal art
Pygmy music
An Amazon sculpture
A Nepalese dance
A Lakota song
A poem by Tagore
The teachings of Buddha
The philosophy of Zen
The sermons of King
The silence of Gandhi

How prejudice begins

A terrorist's bomb
A prisoner's rape
A nameless face

How love turns to hate

A broken promise
A fierce fight
A frightened night

How evil exists

A hatred of humankind
A pleasure in pain
A belief in my god

How god destroys

One man's philosophy
A mystical being
A prophet who speaks

How power turns to terror

An army of killers
A hatred of speech
The rule to decide

How weakness turns to power

When you have no choice
When you know it's time
When you want to make your life matter

For the love of god, country and duty

In the name of god

In the name of god
I will put you to the question and get you to the truth

In the name of god
I will ask you again

İDIME! İDIME!

In the name of god
I will help you remember

In the name of god
I will stretch you out on a rack and pull your flesh out

İDIME! İDIME!

CONFESS! CONFESS!

AYYYYYYYYYYYY DIOS…..AYYYYYYYYYYYY DIOS
SÍ…….I AM A JEW…… SÍ…….I AM A JEW
AYYYYYYYYYYYYYYYYYYYYYYYY

ALLAH
JEHOVAH, YAHWEH
AHURA MAZDA
ELOHIM
ADONAI
EL SHADDAI
BRAHMA, VISHNU, SHIVA
DIOS, DIOS

In the name of god.
In the name of god.

For my country

For my country
I will rape your daughters,
I will kill your sons,
For my country
I will grind your bones,
I will eat your heart,
For my country
I will give my right arm,
I will take your one life,
For my country
I will die ten times over,
I will sacrifice thousands more,
For my country
I will line you up in front of a firing squad and blow your brains out,
I will murder every man, woman and child and bury them in one mass grave,
For my country
I will pay homage to those that die,
I will imprison those that survive,
For my country
I will hang you 'til your neck cracks,
I will hang you 'til your eyes burst,

GERMANY
RWANDA
BOSNIA
CAMBODIA
RUSSIA
JAPAN
TURKEY
SPAIN
ARGENTINA
CHILE
CHINA
DARFUR
AMERICA
AMERICA
AMERICA

For my country.
For my country.

It's my duty

It's my duty
To blood-taint-Taino with el-conquista-doRico,
To blue-gray-Vietnam with purple-heart-graves,
To minute-men-El Paso with foreign-free-fences,
To tazer-speak-Spanish with speak-right-English,
To water-board-Gitmo with don-Jihad-Rumsfeld,
To cleanse-Croat-creed with sanctimonious-Serbian-sperm,
To intera-Tutsis-terror with hamwe-Hutus-hands,

It's my duty.
It's my duty.

Ending it All

Dying alone ain't easy

Dying alone ain't easy
I've done it many times
in the bed
in the shower
on the floor
on the stairs
I've tasted my dimming pulse
I've heard the silence of light
I've felt the attraction of depth
I've wandered free of want
I've sunk deep inside the shining light
In the middle of the night
And all day long
Only to live one more day

Sometimes I'm waiting for the sparrow of death
To start building its nest where I rest

My time has come

I said my time has come
I've said it before
I said my time has come
I'll say it again

You don't believe me
You think it's a lie
You don't believe me
You think it's a fraud

When you get a notion
You just don't bother
You just get that notion
And then you just don't bother

Dying is easy when living is hard
Dying is easy when living is hard

I'm going now
I've got to get on dying

What I owe life is time

Take it from me
Take it away
I can't stop time

Time

Tic Toc
Tic Toc
Ding Dong
Ding Dong
Your life is gone
Time moves on

Time to bow out now

Time to bow out now
In your breasts
In your arms
In your eyes
I can't do you harm

Time for me to leave
I'll call your name
I'll speak your scent
I'll taste your breath
I won't do you harm

Time to disappear
Time is here
There is no more time
In the morning I'll be gone
I mean you no harm